A

AN ARBITRARIUM$_6$ PROJECT

MMXVIII

Monday January 1, 2018

† *Coordinated Universal Time* (UTC) *is the primary time standard by which the world regulates clocks and time. Time zones around the world are expressed using positive or negative offsets from* UTC.

AN IMAGE OF some of the Fa'afafines in Samoa during the celebration of New Year.

This was taken outside of the Mulivai Cathedral Church following the New Year's Eve service whereby hundreds and hundreds of Samoans gathered as tradition.

This service is very important because it brings together families, friends and congregation to worship and acknowledge God's favor for our people over the past year (2017), and to also pray for all the best for the New Year.

+13

In Samoa, this tradition is shared by most. Despite having different plans and activities to welcome the New Year, people begin with the church services held from either 10 PM or 11 PM, and stretching to midnight.

Regardless of negative feedback and finger-pointing towards Fa'afafines—saying we are against biblical teachings and beliefs—the image portrays otherwise.

We also submit this image to share with the world that Fa'afafines have come a long way in terms of earning respect and recognition, and are accepted to dress the way they prefer to attend church services.

The last image reflects the plans and happenings afterwards. Following the church service, the ladies celebrated briefly with their families before returning to their own celebration.

Based on the picture, the Divas sure do know how to have a fabulous time on their own.

The Fa'afafines in the pictures are:

- Lisha Dion
- Barbara Tiufea Vaa
- Shanalei Silva
- Mara Limaauga
- Bell Latulipe
- Liz Lomitusi

All are members of the Samoa Fa'afafine Association. Ⓐ

+13

9

Mum's House
Newtown
7 AM

I JUST HEARD MUM leave for work. My head hurts a little from last night and my eyelids feel like they're stuck to my eyeballs.

It's been a while since I've been home. My Mum still lives in Newtown. We lost the family house a few years back, so now she rents one of my brother's best friend's parent's houses. It's kind of ironic looking down on the place you used to live in from up on the hill. If you stand by the left-hand side of this house, you can see the zoo and its brightly coloured signs amplified by the sounds of animals tucked away behind it. A few hundred metres around the back of this place, you can look out onto the social housing flats where they've jammed all the immigrants and elderly people. It seems they've had an upgrade with the addition of window screens to hide behind, or perhaps keep the residents hidden away from tourists flocking to the zoo.

+12

Last night I had to bury one of the old chickens that live on the property and this morning when I let them out of the coop, the remaining three looked confused.

The weather is a bit shit for summer. Wellington used to be my town, the place where I grew up and where all my friends used to come from. It's funny being a visitor in your own hometown. I don't recognise the shops. There used to be bookstores and opshops, now they've been replaced with barbershops and microbreweries.

the wind cuts through me
this used to be home
I used to think I would never leave
I don't belong here anymore

Felix Café
Corner of Wakefield & Cuba Streets
+12
9:25 AM

I've chosen "toast with homemade jam served with your choice of five grain, sourdough, gluten-free or ciabatta" and ordered a long black.

I'm thinking back to when I was about 18 or 19 and I moved to Auckland. At the time, everyone told me I was making a mistake. Everybody I spoke with talked about how Auckland was too big, too expensive, too trendy, too fast and that I wouldn't last more than a few months. Even my Mum said I'd be back.

By the time I got to Auckland I was miserable and felt out of place. A wall grew around me and I hated the way *Aucklanders* dressed and talked. I'd come home every month, I was never away long enough to let Wellington fade. In my mind Wellington was a friendlier and easier city than Auckland, because *Auckland* was making me miserable. It took moving to a new flat with other people from out of town who loved being in Auckland to realise it wasn't the city's fault I hadn't settled, it was because I'd never wanted to be there in the first place. That small shift changed the way I saw my surroundings—the weather was warmer, and the wind didn't come from Antarctica and knock you down as you walked down the street. People went outside on summer nights and you could swim at the beach three months of the year, not only on the three days that it was warm enough.

I still went home at any opportunity, but four or five times a year instead of every few weeks. I always left early in the morning so that nine hours later I'd arrive at Ngauranga Gorge just before sunset. By the time I wound my way down the winding part of the motorway, I'd see Wellington just as the lights went on in the harbour. It was the best feeling coming home but when it was time to leave I didn't feel so homesick. I had finally settled in Auckland.

One New Year I had some friends drive down to Wellington with me. There were four of us in my tiny white Fiat. I loved showing them the places to go, where to get the best coffee, where to hear the best live music and where to go dancing until 3 AM. Everywhere we went we bumped into old friends that either worked in clubs and cafes or had just finished playing a set. They'd shout my visitors drinks and offered to take them places the next day. After a couple of days, my Auckland friends teased me that Wellington was like a club where "you're in or you're out, but you only know about it when you're out." I laughed, "No way, Wellington is just cool and the people are super friendly!"

Twenty years later and I'm back. I went to bed at 10 PM the night before. After drinking a couple bottles of wine in the kitchen with my mum, she tried to get me to go out and visit my friends. I laughed at her, "What friends? This isn't my town anymore!" 🐦

+11

AWIS

+10

THE BIG EVENT in Sydney for New Year's Eve is the fireworks over the harbour bridge. So popular are they that people camp 48 hours beforehand to ensure they get a good vantage spot. 15 minutes and millions of (tax) dollars worth of fireworks later, the crowd disperses, desperately hoping they can get home before dawn as the main roads are closed and public transport is scarce.

Another tradition is waiting for the MC on the national ABC newscast to screw up and accidentally say something wildly inappropriate. Sure enough, this year he implored the crowds to "kill the police" instead of "kiss the police." Naturally, social media lit up and thus another tradition was upheld.

The first day of the year dawned hot and bright with typical summertime Sydney weather. I went out for a walk along the Parramatta River foreshore to watch children testing out new bikes and scooters on cycling paths while parents were clearly trying to get over hangovers. The bright sunlight was of no help and several looked as if a dive into the river would have been welcome. I sat in my favourite café by the river and enjoyed the sight of sunlight on water and the top of the ANZ Stadium in the distance.

A trip to the local mall, at least, showed a brighter face than it did when I was a child, when every store and restaurant would be closed. Today, families crowded into the Chinese restaurant for *yum cha*, children screamed as they played at the indoor playground and, though a few stores stayed closed, most did a thriving trade undeterred by the public holiday surcharge. There will soon be a time when there is no difference between public holidays and normal days as penalty rates become a thing of the past, and every store and restaurant is encouraged to remain open. While I understand this is not great for retail and restaurant workers who deserve time off as much as the rest of us, I do enjoy being able to shop and eat out on public holidays.

+10

Summertime in Australia means cricket, long hot days that smell of suntan lotion, the gentle sound of ball on bat. What I enjoy the most are the long test matches that can go on for five days, sometimes still no winner at the end. If nothing else, it teaches you to be philosophical.

I love the fact that you can leave the television on in the background for hours, watch the few exciting moments then get back to reading, housework, napping, or even working, and you don't miss anything. That's why many people find cricket boring, but once you understand the tactics and the strategies involved, it can take a lifetime to fully appreciate how fascinating it actually is.

While watching the cricket, I scrolled through social media as friends throughout the world posted photos of themselves celebrating the start of the New Year. I use social media primarily to stay in touch with friends and ex-colleagues who are now scattered all over the world. I love to see what they are doing, congratulate them on major life events and all that stuff, but surely there should be a limit on how many holiday photos can be posted? I don't need to scroll through 50-odd photos of couples all loved-up by the beach. Is it envy, I ask myself? Perhaps a bit.

Social Media Boasting has led to a syndrome called Social Media Envy where you see your friends having a better *'life'* than you. I don't believe that's true—they just know how to use a decent filter. They have just as many problems and concerns (maybe more), but they don't put them on Facebook. No photos of the kids screaming, chucking tantrums, or throwing up. Yet you know it happens on a daily basis. No boasting about how their spouse is working day and night, neglecting them. They post pictures of perfectly-dressed, laughing kids and the flowers the husband bought them "just because …" (though I am very tempted to add "… *he's cheating on you?*").

And maybe that should be my main resolution this year: realise my life is pretty darn good, stop obsessing over how it could be better (especially as I know I burn easily and sand gets everywhere, so photos on the beach are a terrible idea), and just be glad for my friend's happy, social media-appropriate moments.

So I ended the first day of 2018 by pressing 👍Like on her album of 55 pictures, wished her a happy New Year, and resolved to be content. 🐦

+10

+9

I TOOK THIS PICTURE in the Shinkansen, which is the bullet train in Japan.

I was going back to Tokyo to meet my parents.

You can see Mt Fuji from the Shinkansen and I was just waiting for the moment in the vestibule.

It's hard to notice Mt Fuji behind the cloud but the weather was what it was. ✿

WELL I DEFINITELY did not kick-start my New Year with an enthusiastic note, to say the least.

+8

My family and I were slumped against the sofa, eyes dilated, staring at a blaring television. Even the programme was bad—some low-budget, live-streamed, local attempt at a New Year's party, filmed God knows where. Not quite what I had in mind when the idea of celebrating the New Year sprang to mind. I was expecting at least a small gathering with my cousins, or perhaps even watching the fireworks down by Marina Bay Sands with my family. Something, or anything, was better than what I was doing.

I guess I unfortunately started 2018 on an extremely low note. However I think it's unhealthy to carry such negativity into the New Year. After all, it was only a mundane day. I very, very sincerely hope the rest of the year will not disappoint. ▋

THIS IS THE START of a new hope. An arbitrary start, assuredly, but a convenient one. Bizarrely, this new start begins in the past.

The man next to me is shovelling noodles into his face. Looking beyond the languid waters of the Mekong to fishermen readying their longboats, I take a bite of my croissant. This feels very neo-colonial. More than 60 years ago, when Grandpa was here, it was just plain colonial.

He's gone now, but his stories are still with me, taking on the veneer of legend as time pushes the facts further and further away. He didn't win, he couldn't, but he had to fight—it was his job.

He was part of the forces that fought to maintain the supremacy of croissants over noodle soup. It was a doomed struggle, now they coexist here peacefully.

Only at my local, the Café de l'Esplanade, they don't coexist. Marcel would proudly scoff at the very idea, «*jamais de la vie.*» It would be inconceivable. And yet, it might not be. Over his dead body perhaps, but what's to say that the future won't provoke culinary shake-ups like the ones I'm witnessing now. Maybe phở will be as ubiquitous as the Americano I'm sipping.

That's the beauty of this arbitrary new hope. Anything can happen, and today, I can legitimately let my mind wander without being scolded for being a dreamer. We dreamers are troublemakers, so we have to be kept on a leash and dream rationally. We are told to make resolutions.

I've never been one to make resolutions. I'll tell anyone who'll listen that I won't make arbitrary commitments on an arbitrary day. The reality is I lack the discipline to contemplate doing sit-ups or going on a diet, or learning a new language long enough for any of these things to make a noticeable difference.

This year, though, I make a private resolution, like so many have before. I won't share it

+7

with anyone until they can realise for them- selves what's cooking. It will have a poetically uncertain outcome. It will be better than a six- pack, or dropping a waist size, presumably. But the reality is I can't know. In my mind, however, it will be beautiful. The most beautiful. Ever.

I hope I won't have to trudge through the jungle like my grandfather did, but I do hope that I'll have someone to tell his stories to. I'll be able to tell them whatever I want, but I hope I'll stick to facts, as they were recounted to me.

I'm sure the facts I heard weren't the factual facts, but I wouldn't have expected Grandpa to stick to boring old truth. He wasn't like that. He knew that most of life isn't really worth recount- ing, or is too unseemly, and I'm sure he took liberties to make reality more entertaining or palatable. I think I too might use poetic license to fill in the increasingly large gaps. The family history quickly becomes family mythology as a man, normal, but with extraordinary influence over the clan, becomes Zeus through distorted re-telling of familiar stories.

It's only natural that the stories change. Otherwise, the storyteller gets bored. A bored storyteller is a poor storyteller, and no one wants to listen to a poor storyteller. Maybe my audi- ence will tell me: «you've told us that story a million times....» But hopefully, they'll still want to listen. I know I'll want to tell them, over a bowl of phở perhaps. When my resolution comes true. ⁖

+6½

THERE'S NOTHING NEW about the New Year. It $+5\frac{1}{2}$ happens over and over, at the beginning of every year. I know it's not the greatest idea to start off on such a negative note. But my New Year had a predictable start to it so it only seems fitting.

What do you expect from someone from an exotic subcontinent like India? Grand cultural celebrations? Amazing food? I'm sure this was all part of someone's New Year's day. Just not mine.

I am 19 years old and not for long. All my friends were out partying and I was stuck at home playing video games. It felt like a very foul beginning to my last New Year's day as a teenager. I had never been that sick of my life. Here in India, they protect daughters to this annoying level. So if you're wondering why I wasn't out partying, the answer is, I wasn't allowed to.

One reason this night-in felt like such a downer was because things used to be a lot better. I used to feel a lot better about myself. Last year, I drove around town with my dad during the New Year's countdown, and we were joined by the entire city. Everyone was on bikes or in cars cruising around, screaming at the top of their lungs. About a hundred or so strangers wished me a Happy New Year! No one cared about cast or creed. It was just about being happy and spreading joy to anyone who came your way. It was a magical night.

I decided to keep at least some festival spirit alive this year. I stayed up till 12:00 AM then instantly went to bed. Sounds of fireworks and people celebrating on the streets did not help my aching heart. I slept until the afternoon because I had nothing better to do.

I love playing video games. Don't get me wrong here. I just hoped to be doing something a little more outdoors that day.

+5½ Whenever I am down in the dumps, my friend reminds me that life isn't just about the downs. And that once we grow up and have our lives to ourselves, we'll be able to do anything we want. That speech didn't really make anything better. But it did make me want to try.

So I went to visit my sister who'd just had a baby. My very own little niece. She's a ray of sunshine in my otherwise tragically boring life. I figured visiting her might turn things around. It might sound like I'm being dramatic about this whole crappy New Year thing, but you'd get it if you were a teenager too. Sometimes we feel like life isn't fair for no reason at all. I blame it all on the hormonal mood swings.

Being around my sister and brother was a great distraction. Getting to be around the baby, an even better distraction. After I stepped into the room with her crib, it didn't matter what day of the year it was, or whether or not my life was cool.

She was asleep and I sat there looking at her feeling life was perfect all of a sudden. That's when it hit me. Maybe I am just a boring old teenager with no life in this messed up country that gives teenage girls no freedom whatsoever, but here family is everything. No matter how much they suffocate you, they're all you need. I don't think I'd have this bond with so many people if I was from anywhere else. I don't think just holding a baby and realising she's your flesh and blood can mean so much if you're from anywhere else.

Maybe I don't hate my life so much after all. Or maybe I just really like babies.

This pointless story has a happy ending too. While I was lost in her little eyes, the corner of her lips seemed to curve up a bit. I was blabbing random things to her because she liked being talked to. It must have looked crazy. A grown woman talking to a newborn like she could actually make sense of it. I don't even remember what I said. Who knows, I might have been whining about my life to her as well. But whining using my baby voice of course!

+5½

And suddenly she smiled at me. It was her first smile and she decided to let me be at the receiving end of it.

I know what you're thinking, babies that young can't even see. She must have just seen a funny shaped blob and smiled at nothing. But I choose to believe that it was at me. I got all excited and called everyone over to show what just happened. I felt so warm. The warmth trickled from my stomach, down to my pants.

The baby peed on me! I was suddenly thrust into a fountain of never-ending pee. Thankfully it didn't stink. That's my niece, ladies and gentlemen!

So this New Year, I got peed on. I guess I finally got that craziness I was looking for. ◖

+4

+4

ESMAT RABI

+4

–4

NEW YEAR'S DAY was reserved unpacking my suitcase, and cleaning up the apartment. In the afternoon I would treat myself with a restorative trip to the hamam, complete with massage.

+3

But I got back to İstanbul late New Year's Eve and was fairly jet-lagged, so didn't wake up until almost noon on New Year's Day—already the best part of the day gone. Also, a friend and former co-worker who moved to Italy almost two years ago was in town. So I left my suitcase in the middle of the white plastic laminate floor—lying on top of it, the half-unrolled weaving I had brought with me to the US to work on over Christmas holiday. The weaving will be green with a bright orange square, but there needs to be more to it. I've made several sketches, but so far I can't figure it out.

My friend and I met and sat at the back of a café in the neighborhood where she was staying, passing time in conversation. In the spirit of holiday indulgence, we had coffee and dessert. We talked about her life in Italy, what was working out for her, what wasn't. She's always talking about moving back to Turkey but I doubt she will. She likes to savor the idea but I think she fretted so long over whether or not to leave in the first place, and spent so much money and effort actually getting out of here, that it would be a shame to return. And we talked about my life in İstanbul, what's working out, what isn't.

Getting back from vacation is hard. This year I was back with my family on Christmas for the first time in a few years and had a really nice time. Returning to full-time life however, all its conflicts are suddenly thrown into glaring relief: the way it's not making sense, the things you've been in the habit of avoiding. It takes about a week to get back into it.

When I got back home to my apartment, I washed my brunch dishes, and went to bed. 🦇

+3

I WENT ON MY USUAL daily hike this morning and heard the crowned eagles calling.

It's breeding season once again, after a two year gap, for the African crowned eagle (*Stephanoaetus Coronatus*) on Lajuma Research Center in Limpopo, South Africa. This particular eagle is large in stature and has a hawk-like appearance, especially when flying. In flight it shows well-rounded wings and a long, barred-like tail. The underwing is rufous, with the primaries and secondaries heavily barred with black. The female is larger and underwing barring less extensive than on the male. Their habitat consists of evergreen forest and dense vegetation, which makes Lajuma an ideal breeding ground. Breeding only occurs every second year as the parents look after the juvenile for around 6-11 months once the youngster has fledged, teaching it to start catching its own prey and become a supreme, stealth-like hunter.

+2

This pair have apparently been breeding here for many years. When I first arrived, I was made aware there was a juvenile on the nest. I attempted then to view the nest from a cliff approximately 30 metres away, but unfortunately the youngster had just left. Two years later and the pair are rearing another chick, around 12 weeks old. Incubation is about 51 days while the chick takes 110 days to fledge. The same nest has been used for years, repaired during breeding season by both eagles. The female does the majority of the incubation, hunting, and looking after of the chick. The young eagle is estimated to reach breeding maturity at around five years old.

The crowned eagle has a large "menu" to choose from here on the mountain, ranging from rock hyrax, to samango and vervet monkeys. It is considered Africa's most powerful eagle, able to carry heavy prey like ungulates such as duikers. The crowned eagle has large talons

+2

and very strong hindlegs, and can kill its prey by crushing the skull.

The population is decreasing more than previously thought due to the destruction of native tropical African forest. It is estimated that there are only 80 wild breeding pairs in South Africa. It's a realization that, like most endangered species, it is up to us to conserve and protect what's left of these majestic creatures before it's too late. ✒

–2

+1

THE RHYTHM OF this January 1st, 2018 was the rhythm of the raindrops on the windows, on the stairs, on the roof.

Water

Water Water Water Water Water Water Water Water Water Water

Water   *Water*   *Water*

−1

Water

Water

Water

Water

Water

Water

+1

Water, in familiar French, is called *flotte*, which sounds a lot like *flood*.

Our stairs became a waterfall we had to walk through. We had the chance to live next to a beautiful stream.

Living next to moving water reminds me everyday that there is no way to cling to things. Everything is moving, evolving, changing constantly, with every breath. Even if it is hard sometimes to accept, it is also our blessing.

With so much rain, our familiar landscape changed so much. Having my sweet daughter Maya pausing or taking pictures with me was a beautiful way to share this first day of the New Year. 🐦

+1

0

BRANCHES THAT skeined fireworks last night are filigreed grey on grey the first morning of 2018. Cozy next to Mickey in the attic bedroom nest I've hewn from his old flat on the common; snuggled under a magnificent birthday quilt.

The hospital rings. He's on call. Cars swish past on wet pavement, planes whine and roar Heathrow descents. A speakerphone voice describes the symptoms of a dying patient as Mickey prepares for duty.

I join him in the kitchen. On telly, the first glimpse of 2018: a pudgy white guy wearing a suit and two ornamental women, smiling smug at an interviewer. I don't stick around long enough to find out if he's man-on-the-street New Year reveler or budding politician. Dire portent either way.

Escape to the garden, old coat and flip-flops. Our tiny square of nature, one flight down. I pruned olive, yucca and grape yesterday, pulled out dead nasturtiums and montbretia, cleaned leaves from the puddle-pond. The only work I find today is shifting slate onto renegade bamboo. My garden companion of the last couple years watches with a quizzical eye. Fat and healthy. I enquire, but the robin declines having its photo taken for your edification.

0

While shifting slate, a feeling of gratitude settles. For my home, for my recent citizenship in a country more diverse yet equal in rights and opportunity than most others, for my husband, for work that I love that pays more than I need. A life that affords me contentment and security, opportunity to learn and pursue imagination. In the context of history, I am surely one of the very, very few most lucky.

But as the New Year begins, I feel too the loss of optimism.

I remember the years before last and a giddy sense of standing on the brink of great changes. Ecosystems were already collapsing, culture was dominated as always by the most aggressive, power mostly in the hands of those with the least conscience—or perhaps the most ignorance. But within the bloom of technology, a godlike potential for good as well as bad. All knowledge suddenly in the palms of our hands. A miracle of enlightenment unfolding. Humanity waking to consequence and potential.

Surely humans couldn't help evolving, washed sane in the flood of information, convergence of experience and understanding. Learning from our mistakes. Not too late to undo damage we'd done. Not too soon to start imagining what we could achieve.

2017: the year of transition from hopeful concern to resigned mourning. Too late in 2018 to save what I found sacred in our landscapes. No seas unpoisoned, no land unlittered, no air unpolluted. The pristine places where I found my own version of divinity, never to be experienced again.

2017: miracles of knowledge and communication corrupted, twisted away from democratic enlightenment towards weaponised ignorance. Another year of greed ascendant, harvesting its crop of intolerance, violence and fanaticism. A stepping backwards, a forgetting of lessons learnt in war. The year I turned off the news. The year I could lose belief in humanity's ability to navigate its own power.

Under London's cold grey sky (with bit of a hangover) I make a wish for 2018: to find a hope for hope. And some sunlight.

It seems last night the foxes had a bit of a party too. I tidy their detritus of half-chewed plastic.

Mickey comes home with lunch. It's three o'clock. Clouds break on extraordinary blue sky for the last hour of daylight.

As darkness falls I illustrate a historical walking map of our neighbourhood, not quite work and not quite recreation. It occurs to me that the same hope led me to the project as to *Arbitrarium*: that connection brings understanding and all else follows.

The first moon of the New Year rises exceptionally huge and bright, aloof but omnipresent. While I work, Mickey photographs it from the kitchen window with his phone. 🦊

0

-2

HEIDI AND I were good, we didn't go and party. Consequently, we weren't hungover today.

We both had a "work" day, even though we also had company, as a prospective buyer (who is said to be quite wealthy) was expected to visit the farm ASAP.

Like painting the Golden Gate Bridge, as soon as you've done a job on the farm, it's time to start it over again. New Year's Day was a continuation of the battle to contain/control the "green stuff" (vegetation): grasses, tree trimming, etc.

It's a privilege to live here, yet after 10 years there's a lot of stuff you're no longer aware of. Things that should be exciting become day-to-day.

Still, we had a wonderful, wonderful first day of January 2018. Eating mangos from our trees, enjoying the farm. In the afternoon, Daniel—a friend from town—dropped in for a visit. 🐾

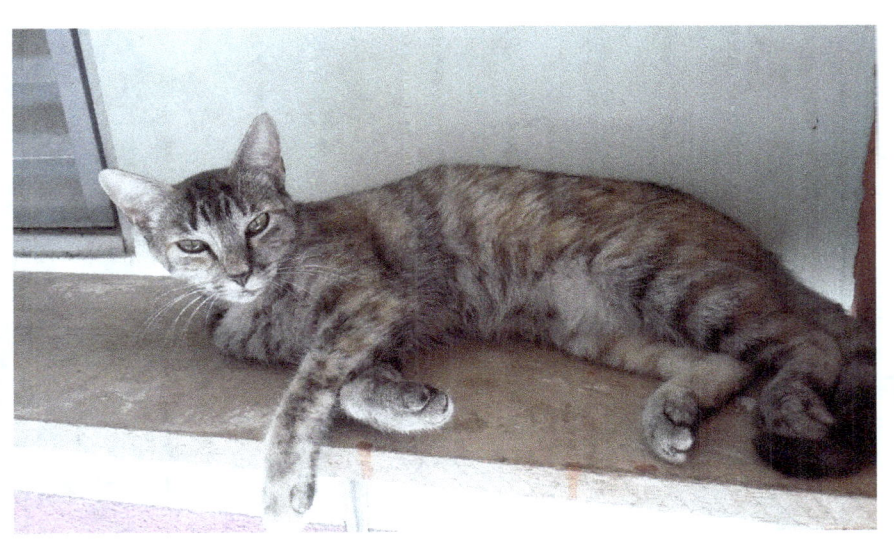

I AM NOT an economist but, fortunately or not, have been working as such for the last few years. My role entails gathering a lot of information in order to make comparisons useful for my company. Have we done better than the year before? If yes, bonuses tend to be bulkier and everyone's happy. Otherwise, we have to find out what happened and make adjustments.

-3

Fantastically, modern capitalism helps to replicate these "business practices" into our daily lives. For example, I have an application on my phone that calculates how my meditation routine is going by telling me how many hours I spent trying to "let go and breathe." Another one tells me how unwisely I spent my salary. I could continue with many examples like this.

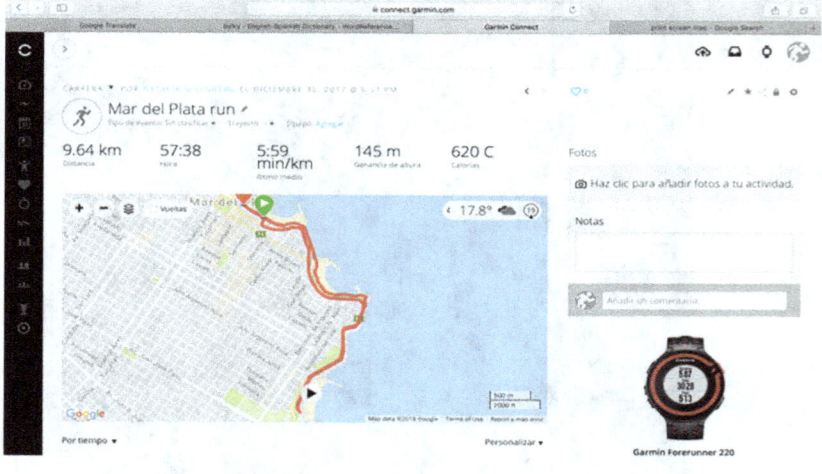

But the gadget that gave me bad news today was my sports watch. It brings me insights on how much I run and, given that it's January 1st, I should be checking my past performance … 25% fewer kilometres than in 2016. Wow! An absolute shame given that running is one of my favourite activities—it keeps me fit and in a good mood.

Now is the right moment of the year to find out what happened and make adjustments so that I can become FITTER, HAPPIER, MORE PRODUCTIVE.

A structured thinking approach would be the following: if it wasn't running, how was this 25% spent? There are two options:

Positively:
- socialising (sometimes this could entail drinking but I won't get into details)
- reading (Goodreads app tells me this is not the case)
- doing yoga (yes, maybe …)
- writing (does explain a little of the 25% given that I started my first creative writing course this year)
- listening to new music on Spotify (actually this could be the case considering my 2017 playlist is enormous and I am quite proud of that)

Negatively:
- eating carbs is the worst alternative to running but I haven't gained weight (tracked on Apple Health)
- Facebooking, Instagraming…? (being jealous of the trips my friends made in 2017 and consuming advertisement)
- watching Netflix (I don't want to know how many hours of my life have been wasted in front of the screen—so I will never know)

–3

My conclusion is that it is impossible to track where this 25% has gone.…

Watching The Tudors on Netflix a few weeks ago, a quote from Henri VIII caught my attention… "Of all losses, time is the most *irrecuperable*, for it can never be redeemed." If he were alive in the 21st century, he would have used the same apps. ✳

THE PERIODIC CYCLES OF THE (*NEW*) YEAR;

or, The Seasons and Their Minutes

* SPRING *

8:57 AM (*bedroom*)—woke up, snoozed alarm, fell back asleep. 9:06 AM—woke up a second time, turned off alarm, & got up. 9:07 AM (*bathroom*)—urinated, flushed toilet, waited for tank to fill, fiddled with handle then flushed again. 9:09 AM (*kitchen*)—started kettle to boil. 9:13 AM—poured water over tea to brew morning pot. 9:14 AM (*bathroom*)—showered: first hot, then cold water. 9:21 AM (*bedroom*)—dressed: dark-khaki chinos, white button-up, & emerald-green cardigan.

"… I'm tired…."

"There's tea in the pot."

"O.K."

9:23 AM (*kitchen*)—poured my first cup of tea. 9:27 AM (*study*)—sat at desk to study. 10:30 AM (*bedroom window sill*)—smoked 1st cigarette of the day. 10:38 AM (*bedroom*)—meditated. 11:08 AM (*kitchen*)—poured out my second cup of tea, emptying pot.

"Do you want me to make another pot of tea?"

"I'll have another cup if you make more."

* *SUMMER* *

11:17 AM (*kitchen*)—started kettle to boil.
11:21 AM (*kitchen*)—poured water over tea to
brew afternoon pot. 11:22 AM (*living room*)—sat
down in chair to read. 12:01 PM (*bathroom*)—
urinated, flushed toilet, finagled handle to stop
tank from running. 12:04 PM (*dining room*)—sat
down at dining room table to work.

"You getting hungry?"

"I could eat soon. Want me to start cooking?"   –5

"Yes, please."

2:46 PM (*dining room*)—ate lunch. 3:17 PM
(*bedroom window sill*)—smoked 2nd cigarette.
3:25 PM (*dining room*)—returned to work.
4:45 PM (*kitchen*)—poured out my third cup of
tea. 4:46 PM (*dining room*)—returned to work.

* *FALL* *

7:38 PM (*bedroom window sill*)—smoked 3rd cigarette. 7:47 PM (*dining room*)—returned to work. 9:30 PM (*living room*)—sat down in chair to read.

"What time do you want to eat dinner?"

"I don't know, maybe around eleven-thirty?"

"O.K. I'll start cooking. What are you thinking?"

-5

"Soup."

"Sounds good."

11:34 PM (*dining room*)—sat down to dinner, offered gratitude to God, ate.

"That was delicious. Thank you for cooking."

"Of course."

"What are your plans for the rest of the evening?"

"I dunno, think I might just read a bit. You?"

"Same."

12:17 PM (*living room*)—sat down in chair -5 to read. 1:01 AM (*study*)—sat down to desk to record day. 1:15 AM (*bedroom window sill*)—smoked final cigarette. 1:22 AM (*bathroom*)—brushed teeth; urinated, finagled handle. 1:30 AM (*bedroom*)—said silently my nightly prayers; layed myself down to sleep. ✵

2018 STARTED WITH fireworks in a public space, just like 2017. However, this time I was in Belmopan instead of Dangriga and without my children. The crowd of 500 or so people including Ifa, a cherished cousin, had just counted in reverse from 20 seconds to zero. The raised stage in the parking lot of the football stadium was in front of us with big speakers stacked side by side and on top of each other. Jamaican reggae singer Tanya Stephens serenaded us while many sang along before the countdown.

2017 was officially the past and we all had the gift of the present to make 2018 whatever we wanted. As quickly as those thoughts came, they went. I took a few shots of my cousin with the fireworks in the background and she returned the favor. The music cranked up as the fireworks ended, then the concert got better. No one cared that it was one of the shortest fireworks displays ever.

My hands were full holding my phone to stream the concert using *Periscope*, as well as my camera to capture moments in stills at a better quality. Tanya sang some crowd favorites, and also spent 25 minutes singing a capella songs people called out from the audience which weren't in her set.

"Numada, we have to get backstage for a pic," my cousin said during the final moments of the show. We passed through a narrow space between the speakers and the wire fence that separated the parking lot from the bleachers to reach backstage. Others had the same idea and we were all informed that pictures would have to wait. We followed the entourage up the bleachers to the VIP section.

The VIP section had snacks and drinks but I didn't pay attention to them. I took pictures of the athletes and fans who stood beside the artist. The Area Representative and sitting Minister of Defense, whose department co-sponsored the concert, was also seated in the VIP section. My cousin and I both took photos with the artist before walking home, four blocks away. We reached home to find my 8-year-old wide awake as the 5-year-old slept. Richie, my adult nephew, served as their babysitter and was enlisted by us to take our picture before we turned in.

The thought that I should preserve the first sunrise of 2018 awoke me at 5:18 AM, three hours after falling asleep. I threw on clothes in the darkness, grabbed my devices, and walked two blocks to the sidewalk of the Ring Road for a clear view of a picturesque sunrise. The Ring Road is the oval-shaped street in the center of Belmopan which has seen heavy infrastructural upgrades to ensure the safety of runners and cyclists. I turned on my phone and began live-streaming sunrise via *Periscope*. For about 20 minutes I watched a cloudy dawn turn into a cloudy sunrise as viewers from around the world bid me Happy New Year or expressed appreciation of the view. A dear friend happened to be walking along the Ring Road on his way to work and we exchanged greetings close to the start of my 'scope. He mentioned that he didn't go out because of the recent killing of a friend who may have been targeted because he was gay. The young man was killed while house swapping with a friend in Belize City, while she stayed in his home 3 hours away in the town of Dangriga. My mind drifted to a regional meeting I recorded in November in which a transsexual activist challenged her fellow LGBTQI activists to protest acts of discrimination or hate against all members of the community, not just their subset. I chose not to give the viewers context about the killing but instead focused on the clouds and sunrise.

The rest of the day was like a Sunday, which consisted of rest, playing, and preparing for the workweek. As with sunrise, I took deliberate photos of the first sunset and full moon of the New Year. The moon was a glowing yellow and the clouds seemed conspired to hide it. At about 7:30 PM the moon was so brilliant I called my sons outside so my nephew could take pictures of us with the moon. I remember feeling like the full moon was a good analogy for the full possibilities ahead in this New Year. ◐

-6

-7

THIS ISN'T THAT off-the-shelf eggnog. Sugary, heavily nutmegged (or probably not, it's probably extract), yellow to suggest authentic yolk, consistency of glue, so forth.... Not the stuff you have to cut so deeply with rum and cheap brandy that, unless you take your rum and cheap brandy neat, you'll hate what you're drinking even more than if it were just eggnog off the shelf, straight out of the carton in the store.

This is my eggnog; I won't be alienated from eggnog anymore. Figure, people have been enjoying eggnog since time immemorial, there has to be something to it, right? It's even got the word "nog" in it, that's gotta be Middle English at the latest, hmm?

These are the things we ask ourselves, likely because there's usually a reward for an answer, or even just a semblance of an answer. Now and then, you'll get a topic like eggnog, and do this research—scientific, call it what it is—that culminates in both pain avoidance and pleasure. We usually just get one or the other.

Right then. So it's brandy and rum, cream, whole milk, eggs, some sugar, tiny pinch clove, big pinch cinnamon, and a bunch of nutmeg. Needless to say, spices fresh ground are preferable. First time I made this, I did it in a blender, thereby cooking the eggs and agitating the cream into butter. I didn't taste it, so I can't tell you whether or not it was good; I threw it out mainly because my vision of eggnog did not comport with this creation.

Mix in a bowl, good enough. In fact, that's probably how it's been done for centuries.

It's essentially a perfectly legal speedball, this eggnog: protein overload from the eggs, tryptophan metabolizing into serotonin from the milk and cream, sugar buzz, and alcohol buzz (which, I know, technically, that's a sugar buzz too, but I'm dangerous on eggnog, so you should leave me alone). I'd recommend trying just one mugful. Hold yourself to that for at least an hour, otherwise you'll either fall asleep or try to tease Erdogan into a fistfight from your patio. If you think you can handle more, do it. I care of course, don't want you to hurt yourself. But, you know, do what you want.

And now I take my seat facing east, it comes from the east. I don't smoke anymore (New Year's resolution to quit for many years, and now I'm done with resolutions altogether, more poisonous than a cigarette) so all I'll be holding is my mug of eggnog when it gets here.

I suppose we could do the whole degree of longitude is the cosine of the degree of latitude times a degree of longitude at the equator then measure out to the east end of the time zone, but even that is rough. Earth keeps slowing down a little in both rotation and orbit, the Moon is in a different phase and at a different distance than years prior, the Sun moved, the Milky Way Galaxy moved, then at the bottom we'll find how silly the concepts of latitude and longitude are because as I wrote that everything changed again, and again, and again.

All I'm going to do is take a town roughly on my latitude at the edge of the Mountain Time Zone, get the rough distance between here and that town, do rough conversions, get the rotation of Earth at this latitude in MPH, get midnight at my position precisely, approximately. And I'll laugh at the revelers on television, and tell them, it ain't Midnight yet you sots! Then I'll look at my watch, and when it's actually midnight, not too far away, I'll turn around to the teevee and say, okay now it's okay.

Now it's okay: Happy New Year.

I've seen this attributed to everybody: 'To measure is to know.' Archimedes, Kelvin, some jackass at the Chicago School, everybody. It's likely from a scientist, however defined at the time, needing as we do some explanation of and control over those things not human that ate our ancestors with their sharp teeth and their bitter cold. I say that because a poet of those various times would've said something more along the lines of, 'To measure is to begin to know,' recognizing as they do the unceasing flux.

Not far from here is the NIST, the keepers of the United States' time, temperature, mass, distance ... as precisely as they can. They have a nonreactive metal pound, so it'll be a pound for a while, and they take the time from a hunk of Cesium? Maybe? Let me look ... I'll be damned, it is Cesium, it radioactively decays at the most reliable interval anybody's come across. Not sure how it's done, but they sell clocks at the drugstore tuned to the Cesium.

I tell you this from experience: if you walk into the NIST main building and ask for the time, they'll tell you they don't

-7

know and quit making fun. By the time you'd asked for the time and the interlocutor gave you an answer, several seconds will have passed, so the answer will be incredibly imprecise, and this is not to mention radioactive decay is also inexact, and our inertial frames of reference will never coincide. Here, you have to start talking with Buddhists, poets, and the happier of the quantum physicists.

Midnight January One is the one moment per Gregorian Year we Western people state something is fixed and permanent, then immediately admit it's not. There will be a kiss and a June some immeasurable time in the future. We all know it's rough as hell, and that ball dropping, it indicates nothing, it's wobbly and it gets stuck now and then. Figure, though, at least as far as we're concerned, that's some of what keeps the species worth saving: we have sufficient grace to say good enough. ✿

-7

I learned today that one of my best friends

has never eaten an orange. . . . . e v e r.

This strikes me as odd, like really odd.

Maybe cuz oranges are so common place.

And what about scurvy?

"I tried once, it's consistency was too much like meat,

like it couldn't decide if it wanted to be a fruit or a meat."

Apples, bananas, mangoes, all good. But citrus fruits are off limits.

No grapefruits, no tangerines, no lemons.

But juice form is ok.

I learn this because of the orange zest she adds

to the cupcake frosting she's making.

Seeing the discarded orange on the kitchen counter

I ask what she's gonna do with it.

"Throw it out," she replies and I ask why not eat it?

"I've never eaten an orange."

The only fruit I ate today was an orange.

I eat the unwanted orange, which brings my count up to two.

She laughs.

After all these years we can still find out new things about each other.

And it's funny to think about the impossibility of knowing

another person completely.

NEW YEAR'S DAY HAS always been a transcendent day for Kate Troll, my honey, and me. A day to burn any bitterness from the previous year to ashes, accept and happily remember those loved ones we have lost, and turn our eyes to the future, to what we want our world to be. There's bittersweetness in there; and hope; and joy.

I awake at 7:20 AM, very late for a guy who normally jumps out of bed between 4:30 and 5:00 AM. Kate and I danced until after midnight, hours of big band followed by an hour and a half of raucous, crazy, wonderful rock & roll: New Year's Eve and one day into our 41st year of marriage.

So, I suppose my day really started dancing to rock & roll, toasting in the New Year (non-alcoholic sparkling water for me), followed by my quiet wind-down at home until 2:00 AM.

I awake thinking of our friend, Michelle Ridgeway, a passionate marine ecologist and conservationist, fatally injured in a car crash in Juneau on December 30, only 54 years into a life of ocean exploration, diving from Southeast Alaska to the Arctic.

I gaze out the window above the kitchen sink to check the wind direction and speed—from the south, 15 to 20 MPH. White-capped waves slop right-to-left in my view. So the weather forecasters were right, we're changing from the biting 9° F of yesterday to eight inches of snow overnight ... and then *rain*. Already 29.6° F.

Juneau is a ribbon of humanity etched into the shoreline of Southeast Alaska between the Pacific Ocean and the Coast Range, mountains that fly skyward from sea level to 6,000 feet, the last toehold of North America before sailing west into the Pacific Ocean. Much of the city is less than five streets wide along the coast. End-to-end, the road is only about 60 miles long, with no connection to anywhere else. We travel by ferry to a road that leads elsewhere, or by airline if we're in a hurry. Often, I think this isolation brings friends closer together here.

I need to come to grips with the loss of Michelle. For me, healing from grief always starts in one of my favorite landscapes. Sometimes

-9

I drive the road to Eagle Beach and walk far out onto the exposed tidelands, not caring if the tide catches me. What does it matter if I have to wade back through hip-deep saltwater? I find a special release of my grief when the cold water hits me.

Today, I want to cross-country ski. Hopefully the lake at the foot of Mendenhall Glacier will retain enough cold to give me good snow before the rain starts to fall. I arrive around 10:30 AM with Nellie, our 10-year-old Sheltie puffball of a dog. The snow is too warm, impossibly slippery, and I detest sticky warm-snow ski waxes. So skiing is out.

Nellie and I return to the car, where she patiently watches me change my paws into hiking boots. Out again along the edge of the lake toward Nugget Falls. On such a day, exposed ice in the crevasses of the glacier gleams a lovely deep blue against the gray sky. I stop about half way to the falls, simply stand watching the glacier, let my tears fall.

That deep blue in the ragged crevasses, a portal into the heart of the glacier, gives me peace and joy, a sense of the same toughness and determination I loved in Michelle, a celebration of her quest to understand the deep ocean. In 2007, she piloted a one-person submarine 1700 feet down into the Zhemchug Canyon, a canyon in the Bering Sea that is both longer and deeper than the Grand Canyon, one of five scientists to explore the depths in the first recorded scientific foray into the canyon system.

Nellie has been patiently waiting while I stare at the glacier. Now she gives a yip, then a bark. "C'mon, let's get going." She's a spinner, this Sheltie. And a sneezer. She sneezes hard. Then sneezes again. I've heard that African hunting dogs sneeze to excite their packs into hunting forays. Apparently, Nellie is a cousin … well, a long, long, long, lost cousin.

Perhaps Michelle's most lasting legacy will be the fascination and joy of the children she introduced to the wonders of the ocean, of marine organisms, of the natural world … in coastal Alaskan communities wherever she worked; many many communities.

Nellie spins around, sneezes, barks.

I laugh at her. "Okay. I'm done. Let's hike!"

We walk along the shore of the frozen lake. A drizzly rain begins to fall, but it doesn't matter. The weight in my chest lifts as the clouds settle in, a balancing of loving the world as it is and accepting that which we cannot change, a rejoicing in the deeper blue of the ice and my good fortune to have been on the planet with Michelle. ✹

-9

–10

THE WIND RATTLING the windows woke princess *K*ate while it was still dark out. She stretched her legs on the cool sheets and pointed her toes, thinking about what to do: *go back to sleep or not?*

Trying to be cat-quiet, she lowered herself down from the giant bed, crossing the fingers of her right hand behind her back so she wouldn't wake princess Ella up. Without making a sound, *K*ate crept across the carpet, listening to the creaks and moans of the old house. *This is a fierce wind,* she thought. *I'll go see if the babies are scared.*

In the next room, *K*ate peered over the edge of a crib, not sure if she was looking at princess *C*harlotte or princess *C*aroline. The twins were copies of each other, and in the dim light from the china-lantern nightlight it was impossible to tell who was who. Princess *C*harlotte-or-*C*aroline was awake, and straining her little head up like a turtle to look at *K*ate. She smiled her toothless smile and *K*ate smiled back with her eyes (because not everyone smiles with their mouths).

An idea came into *K*ate's head. "Should we go see what's out there?" *K*ate asked, looking towards the enormous wooden doors that led to the yard. Princess *C*harlotte-or-*C*aroline squeaked softly. As *K*ate reached into the crib, the baby grabbed tightly onto her sister's long golden hair. The other baby was awake now, trying to roll over onto her back, reaching little starfish hands up to *K*ate.

-10

One baby in each arm, tiny fingers entwined in her hair, *K*ate gingerly (*because the babies needed to be carried carefully!*) walked towards the dark wooden exit. There was a whistling noise coming from a crack between the doors.

*K*ate stopped short, head cocked, because she heard a muffled crash followed by a feral wailing across the hall. She sighed and turned toward the noise, resigning herself to taking princess *E*lla with them after all. *E*lla's small figure appeared in the doorway of the other bedroom, backlit from the lamp she had probably turned on and then knocked over. Her halo of glowing hair looked especially wild, pale curls obscuring one eye, while the other eye gave a desperate wink. Ella's white nightgown was too long, lace trim skimming her feet. She was chewing the tip of one of the satin ribbons that decorated the neckline, tears making wet trails down her face.

"Ella," Kate whispered, "Will you help us? We need you to open the big wooden doors because we want to go outside."

Kate was pleased with her cleverness when Ella's face changed as suddenly as if a cloud blew over, the sun shining once again. Wiping her cheek with the back of a frilly cuff, Ella bolted past Kate with a grin, nearly knocking her and the babies over. Kate waited patiently, a baby in each arm, as Ella fumbled with the complicated handle, grunting as she pushed and shoved the big slabs of wood until there was a small-child sized opening. And then, like a dragonfly, princess Ella flew off into the night. Kate followed slowly, hoping that Ella would have the sense

not to get hurt on whatever climbing/swimming/burrowing adventure she got up to.

Kate was the oldest princess. She would have liked to call herself the queen, but obviously her mom was the queen and that was that. There really should be a better name for the first and oldest princess though. Something like *big princess* or *princess master*.

-10

Ella was the middle sister/princess. She was a wild thing. From the moment she woke up until the moment she fell asleep (which happened in random places at odd times, without warning and as if someone had suddenly unplugged her), Ella did not stop moving. She bounced when she ate, ran when she talked (which was a lot and in a rather annoying voice, Kate thought), and was always rolling, climbing, jumping, dancing or just *moving*. If for some reason you didn't sense her constant frenzied movement around the house, chances were that she was up to something bad, like a knife drawer or Dad's computer. Ella halted or at least slowed down when she was doing something that was *off limits, even for a princess,* so stillness around her was a warning of danger. Kate thought Ella naughty and unpredictable, if she was being honest. Calling her sister a wild thing was just a polite way of saying Ella was actually quite dangerous, and best avoided whenever possible.

The littlest princesses, Charlotte and Caroline, on the other hand, were perfect. In the glossy moonlight Kate could now see who was who. In her right arm was Caroline, whose silky hair had two circle patterns on the top of her head. Mom had said they were called *whorls,* which must be the word for hair circles. Charlotte only had one whorl, at the back-bottom part of her head, and the hair on the top formed a straight line. Mom said that was called a *mohawk,* which must mean hair straight-line.

Kate once asked Mom why the babies had

-10

86

different shapes in their hair while all the other parts of their bodies—tiny noses and toes and soft green-colored eyes and even dimples on their plump cheeks—were exactly the same. Mom said the twins' bodies were made the same at the beginning, but they sat differently in Mom's belly, and the way Caroline's head rested on the inside of Mom's belly made two hair circles, and Charlotte's head leaned in a way that made a hair-line instead. Mom also said that every person in the world has teeny-tiny lines on their fingers called *fingerprints,* and no two people ever have the same shapes on their fingertips. Caroline and Charlotte had different fingerprints too, because their little hands had been touching the inside of Mom's belly in different ways. Kate had not yet been able to discern the babies' fingerprints, their fingers were too little.

-10

The yard was a mess because of the wind: chaise lounge cushions were strewn on the lawn, a lantern was knocked over, and there were a ton of what looked like pink blossoms from the Monkeypod tree scattered across the grass and the tiles around the pool.

As Kate surveyed the scene, there was a loud crash and then a splash and a wail from the direction of the swimming pool.

"It sounds like your wild sister is up to wild things," Kate murmured over the tops of the twins' heads. She started walking slowly (*must always be careful carrying the babies!*) towards the edge of the lawn, where there was a big bony tree and cliffs that hung over the ocean. The grass was very cold and very wet, but Kate felt strong. The moon was like a magnet that pulled up her eyes, and also the babies' mossy green eyes. They all looked up, physical bodies fixed into their spot on the lawn.

As Kate stood, mesmerized by the magnetic moon and the light it cast on the glittering ocean, the twins talked to each other. They had a special way of wrinkling their noses and moving their eyes and sticking out their tongues and making little squeaking noises that was private and sophisticated. Normally Kate had no idea what they were saying to each other, but tonight in the moonlight she understood perfectly:

"Happy New Year, princess Charlotte."

"Happy New Year, princess Caroline." 👑

-10

88

TOSH AHKIT has a social practice focused on the reclaiming and activation of new social spaces for individual and collective expression. Her writing is centered on belonging and the ability to be an authority on one's own lived experiences. An example of this is her ongoing collaboration with the Auckland Central Homeless Community through the creation of Radio NFA (No Fixed Abode). *www.toshahkit.com*

EAMON ATLEY lives in New York, where he spends most of his time reading.

PETER BOYCE lives in İstanbul, Turkey. He studies textile art and languages.

FELENE M. CAYETANO is a Belizean Garifuna author, mother, publisher, librarian and editor. She lives in Belize where she advocates for cultural continuity, literacy, authors, poets and small publishers.

CHRISTINE DOMINÉ is a school teacher in rural Belgium and wife of Nathaniel's childhood friend. Her daughter MAYA has just turned 10.

CRISTIÁN FAÚNDEZ is a 37 year old advertising professional who lives in the coastal city of Viña del Mar, some 74 miles northwest of Santiago, Chile's capital. He works as an advertising, marketing, design consultant and as a university teacher.

ABIRAMI GIRI is a writer by day and reader by night—on the whole, a teenage blogger from the city of Coimbatore in the southern parts of India. She started writing poetry in her early teens and has been blogging for over three years. *theobsessivewriter.com*

WILLIAM ARTHUR HANSON is a landscape, wildland lifestyle, and nature writer in Juneau, Alaska. He shares his outdoor adventures and 40 years in Alaska as a biologist, forester, and lover of landscapes through his Alaska Billy Blog and as an Instagram blogger *@bhfootloose.*

TODD HONMA is from San Francisco. He enjoys oranges and he is vegan, so their supposed meat-like texture is lost on him.

RYAN KHOO is a student and nephew by marriage to Nathaniel.

TAKAHIRO KOHIYAMA is a photographer based in Kyoto, Japan.

BERTRAND LANDEL grew up and lived in France, the US, Germany, the UK and Belgium and now lives in Switzerland. He has a day job and loves to eat, cook, travel, read, and is a sometime-blogger. *bertrandabroad.wixsite.com/abroad/blog*

CONNIE LAU is a 30-something year old girl who loves exploring and traveling the world.

NAW WUT YEE LAY is a student in Yangon, contacted through a long chain of friends.

Heidi and DYLAN MACHADO live in a peaceful environment with a spectacular observation of nature—the rural interior of Brasil. Dylan is originally from California and is Nathaniel's uncle.

JOSHUA MCDANIEL defines himself as a Yankee sot. He and Nathaniel were at college together.

NATALIA NIRENBERG came to *Arbitrarium* through Walrus, an English bookstore in Buenos Aires, Argentina, where she attends a creative writing course.

ESMAT RABI is a photographer based in Dubai. She explores the boundaries of visual story-telling through a combination of documentary & fine art photography.

MÁRIO ROBERTO is a visual artist (photography, painting, installation, video) in Ponta Delgada, the main town of the Azores where he has his studio and art gallery. He was born on São Miguel Island.

JOE SALAS enjoys jogging in Central Park in the summertime, collecting Astor Piazzolla records, and Japanese whiskey. His spirit animal is the manatee.

Ymania Brown, Vaialia Iosua and Kevin Schuster all helped with Samoa's submission. They were contacted through the SAMOA FA'AFAFINE ASSOCIATION, whose events Nathaniel had been lucky enough to attend.

KYLE STUART is a friend of friends. He lives and works at a remote nature preserve in the northwest of South Africa. LEIGH is Kyle's sister, now living in London. Her boyfriend, SAM, proposed to her while visiting with Kyle over the New Year's break.

I. WALL lives on the island of Hawai'i and takes care of other people's children, both royalty and commoners alike.

NATHANIEL WALTERS-KOH works in film and TV in the UK.

APIA WILLIE is one of seven artists in the art collective Awis Artis Blong Vanuatu.

JOYCE WONG has previously worked as a reporter and editor and currently works in public relations, specialising in social media strategy. In her spare time, she writes fan fiction for fun and loves reading old-fashioned girls school stories.

ISBN 9781734686708

The cover image is a detail of Apia Willie's *Villej
Niuyia*.

Layout and things done by Joe Salas.

This is the sixth Arbitrarium, published in the spring
(northern latitudes, anyway) of 2018. Much love
and thanks to: Felene Cayetano, Todd Honma, train
delays on the New York City subway, Astor Wines &
Spirits, Aeropuerto de Gran Canaria (for the lovely
sandwiches), Robert Bringhurst, John Coltrane, and
most especially the kindness and generosity of all
contributors.

Joe Salas and Nathaniel Walters-Koh are the
editors-at-large. We accept presents of Gitane
cigarettes, chocolates, and whiskey. And we would
love to hear from you!

arbitrariumzine@gmail.com

"You're the white swan in my photograph."

Ω

www.ingramcontent.com/pod-product-compliance
Lightning Source LLC
Chambersburg PA
CBHW071133100726
47908CB00008B/2587